To my wonderful family - *Chika, Kanayo and Chudi* - whose ever-present love and unwavering support have shown me what it means to live a beautiful life.

The Amazing Pet Year Book

(CLASS OF 2024)

INSPIRING STORIES OF COURAGE AND GOODNESS FOR LITTLE KIDS WITH BIG HEARTS

A.J. CHIVUZO OFFIAH

My name is

_____

I am strong, bold, brave and super-duper amazing. And with the help of my mum and dad, I am going to be the most awesome kid ever.

On this date

_____

I got this wonderful book. You can't imagine how excited I am!
I am so happy!

Introduction

"Even the smallest voice can make a big difference. Speak up for what's right."

Thank you for picking up this enchanting yearbook for the Class of 2024. In the pages that follow, you'll embark on a heartwarming journey of getting to know the extraordinary young pets of this class, each possessing a unique and shining virtue. These are not just any pets; they are the heroes of everyday life, proving that small actions can have a profound impact.

Within the colorful and captivating pages that await you, you'll meet Jason, the Kindhearted Leader, and his remarkable friends who embrace virtues like compassion, curiosity, creativity, and friendship. These stories aren't about capes and superpowers; they are about the superpowers of the heart, showcasing the magic of kindness, empathy, and the joy of learning.

As you turn the pages of this book, you'll find yourself immersed in the stories of these young heroes, learning about their exceptional qualities and the values that guide their lives. You'll witness the power of compassion as they show care for one another, the wonders of curiosity as they explore the world with boundless enthusiasm, and the joy of creativity as they paint their stories with vibrant imagination.

Each story in this book is a testament to the remarkable potential that resides within every child, reminding us that even the smallest gestures can create ripples of positivity. These stories serve as an inspiring reminder that virtues like kindness, perseverance, and empathy can light up the world.

So, open your heart and your imagination as you step into the world of these little but mighty heroes. Let their tales inspire you, warm your heart, and remind you that the greatest adventures often begin with a simple act of kindness. Through these pages, we hope to ignite the virtues in all of us, young and old, and show that every child can be a hero in their own way, leaving a trail of goodness in their wake.

As we embark on this delightful journey, may you be encouraged to embrace the virtues that define these little heroes and, in doing so, discover the magic of kindness, compassion, and the boundless potential within your own heart.

Jason

"Kindness is a superpower. Use it often."

Meet Jason, the pet with a heart as big as a hug and a smile that could brighten the darkest day. As we look back on our year, we can't help but be inspired by his incredible kindness and compassion. Jason's boundless enthusiasm for helping others truly sets him apart.

Jason's superpower is kindness! He's the first to offer a hand when someone needs it, and he's always ready with a comforting word or a friendly hug. Whether it's sharing his crayons or cheering up a friend, Jason shows us all how a little kindness can go a long way.

Jason is an amazing friend who loves to share the magic of stories. He can turn the most ordinary day into an extraordinary adventure with his vivid imagination and enthusiasm for reading.

Jason, your kindness and imagination make our year so much better. You remind us that being a friend and using our imagination can make every day a memorable adventure. Thank you for being our Kindness King and the best dragon-hunting buddy ever!

Ethan

"Life is full of adventure, and you are the hero of your story."

Ethan is the adventurer of our class. He's always up for exploring new places and discovering hidden treasures. His courage and determination remind us that every day is a new adventure waiting to happen.

Ethan's bravery is unmatched! Whether it's climbing the tallest slide at the playground or venturing into the unknown territory of the forest, he's always ready for an exciting journey.

Ethan organized the most epic treasure hunt at his birthday party. We followed clues and discovered hidden gems all around his backyard. It was a day filled with adventure and excitement!

Ethan, your fearless spirit shows us that life is an incredible journey filled with wonders to explore. Thank you for being our Fearless Explorer and reminding us to embrace every new day as an adventure!

Lily

"Every day is a fresh start. Make it a good one."

Lily's imagination knows no bounds! She's our go-to artist, always ready to turn a blank page into a colorful masterpiece. Her creative spirit reminds us that every day is a canvas waiting to be filled with wonderful adventures.

Lily's creativity inspires us all! She loves to paint rainbows, make up stories about magical lands, and turn ordinary rocks into sparkling treasures. Her artful mind shows us that creativity is the key to making the world a more beautiful place.

Who could forget the amazing art show Lily put on in the classroom? Her paintings of rainbows and unicorns made everyone feel like they were in a dream world. We all got to be artists for the day and create our own masterpieces.

Lily, your creativity lights up our world. You show us that with a little imagination, we can turn the ordinary into something extraordinary. Thank you for being our Creative Captain and an inspiration to us all!

Mia

*"In a world where you can be anything,
be kind."*

Mia is our class's heartwarming friend. She's always there with a comforting hug and a listening ear. Her kindness and empathy remind us of the importance of being there for each other.

Mia's kindness shines bright! She's the first to comfort someone who's feeling down or to help a friend who's in need. Mia shows us that a little bit of love can make a big difference.

Mia organized a special friendship picnic for our class. We all brought our favorite snacks, and Mia brought flowers to make it extra beautiful. It was a day filled with laughter, love, and lots of yummy treats.

Mia, your caring nature warms our hearts. You remind us that true friendship is about being there for each other and spreading kindness. Thank you for being our Caring Captain and making our days brighter with your love and flowers!

Noah

"There's nothing you can't do if you set your mind to it."

Noah is our problem-solving superstar. When challenges arise, he's quick to find solutions and make everything better. His determination and resourcefulness remind us that there's a solution to every problem.

Noah's problem-solving skills are legendary! Whether it's figuring out a tricky puzzle or helping build a fort, he's the one to turn to when we need a hand.

Noah loves building with blocks and creating amazing structures. He even built a spaceship in our classroom, and we all got to be astronauts for a day!

Noah led the way in creating the most amazing fort in the classroom. We all pitched in, and it turned into the coziest reading nook ever.

Noah, your problem-solving superpowers show us that challenges are just opportunities to find solutions. Thank you for being our Mighty Problem-Solver and turning every problem into an exciting adventure!

Emma

"You are unique and special, just like a star in the sky."

Emma is the sunshine of our class. Her positivity and laughter are contagious, brightening even the cloudiest days. Her joyful spirit reminds us that happiness is a choice we can make every day.

Emma's happiness is like a ray of sunshine! She's always ready with a smile and a cheerful greeting, making everyone around her feel happier.

Emma loves to dance and can turn any song into a dance party. She's got the most fantastic dance moves and loves to share the joy with her friends.

Emma organized an awesome dance-off during recess one day. We all joined in, showing off our craziest dance moves. It was a day filled with laughter and fun!

Emma, your cheerful spirit reminds us that happiness is a choice, and a smile can brighten anyone's day. Thank you for being our Cheerful Captain and spreading joy wherever you go!

Oliver

"Dream big, little one. Your dreams can take you anywhere."

Oliver is our class's Earth protector. He's always ready to pick up litter, save the planet, and remind us how important it is to take care of our environment.

Oliver's love for the environment is inspiring! He's the first to suggest recycling, reducing waste, and teaching us all to be eco-conscious.

Oliver has a green thumb and grows the most delicious fruits and vegetables in his garden. He even brought some fresh veggies to share with the class!

Oliver organized an Earth Day celebration for our class. We planted trees, learned about recycling, and even made bird feeders to help our feathered friends.

Oliver, your commitment to the environment reminds us to take care of our beautiful planet. Thank you for being our Eco Hero and teaching us how to be Earth-friendly superheroes!

Ava

"Believe in yourself, and you can achieve anything."

Ava is our go-to friend when we need assistance. Her helpful nature and willingness to lend a hand remind us of the power of kindness and being there for one another.

Ava's helpfulness knows no bounds! She's always ready to assist a friend, whether it's tying shoelaces, sharing school supplies, or offering a comforting word.

Ava is known for her incredible baking skills. She often brings delicious treats to share with the class, making our days extra sweet!

Ava organized a cupcake decorating contest, and we all got to be mini bakers for the day. The classroom was filled with colorful cupcakes, laughter, and frosting!

Ava, your helpful spirit reminds us of the joy in lending a hand and making the world a better place. Thank you for being our Helpful Heart and filling our days with kindness and cupcakes!

Liam

"Don't be afraid to be yourself; you are amazing just as you are."

Liam is our natural leader. His courage and determination in the face of challenges inspire us all to be brave and never give up, no matter what.

Liam's bravery is remarkable! Whether it's leading a game, trying a new activity, or facing tough puzzles, he's always ready to take the lead.

Liam is an amazing storyteller. He often weaves captivating tales filled with adventure and imagination, taking us on incredible journeys with his words.

Liam led us on a brave adventure story during a rainy day indoors. We all played different characters and embarked on a quest to save the day.

Liam, your fearless leadership shows us that being brave and determined can lead to incredible adventures. Thank you for being our Fearless Leader and guiding us through the wonderful stories of life!

Hey hey,

Are you enjoying the book so far? Are you learning about being kind, brave and creative?

If yes, then that's awesome! How about you write down two ways you're going to show kindness to your classmates.

_____

_____

_____

_____

_____

Sophia

"Every accomplishment begins with the decision to try."

Sophia is always ready for the next exciting adventure. Her boundless enthusiasm and curiosity remind us to embrace every moment with open arms.

Sophia's enthusiasm is infectious! Whether it's going on a nature walk, conducting science experiments, or learning about new things, she's always eager to dive in.

Sophia has an amazing collection of seashells from all her beach trips. She loves to share interesting facts about each one and even lets us listen to the ocean in them.

Sophia organized a nature scavenger hunt, and we all explored the schoolyard to find hidden treasures. It was a day filled with excitement and discoveries.

Sophia, your enthusiasm for life teaches us to see the world with wonder and curiosity. Thank you for being our Enthusiastic Explorer and inspiring us to embrace each day as a grand adventure!

William

"You have within you the strength, the patience, and the passion to reach for the stars to change the world."

William is our sports superstar. His dedication to sports and determination to keep trying, no matter what, reminds us to be resilient and never give up.

William's athletic spirit is inspiring! Whether it's racing on the playground, scoring goals, or perfecting new moves, he's always ready for action. William is great at sharing tips and tricks about sports. He loves teaching his friends how to kick a soccer ball, shoot hoops, and more!

William organized a mini Olympics event for our class. We had a relay race, a soccer tournament, and even a trophy for everyone who participated. It was a day filled with sportsmanship and fun!

William, your fearless athleticism shows us that with practice and determination, we can achieve our goals. Thank you for being our Fearless Athlete and inspiring us to stay active and resilient every day!

Grace

"You are a shining star, and your light brightens the world."

Grace is our class's music magician. Her love for making melodies and sharing her musical talents remind us of the joy that music brings into our lives.

Grace's music is like magic! Whether it's playing the piano, singing sweet songs, or creating lovely beats, she's always ready to make our days more melodic.

Grace often organizes mini concerts during recess where she shares her musical talents with the class. It's like having our own private music show!

Grace organized a musical talent show for our class. Everyone got a chance to showcase their musical talents, from playing instruments to singing. It was a day filled with harmony and applause.

Grace, your musical magic reminds us that the world is a better place with the sound of music. Thank you for being our Musical Maestro and making our days more harmonious and joyful!

Benjamin

"It's okay to make mistakes; that's how we learn and grow."

Benjamin is our inquisitive scientist. His love for experiments and discovery reminds us of the magic that happens when we ask questions and explore the world around us.

Benjamin's curiosity is boundless! Whether it's conducting science experiments, asking "why" and "how," or showing us cool facts, he's our resident scientist. He often brings in fascinating objects from nature, like cool rocks and leaves, to show the class. He loves to share interesting facts about them.

Benjamin organized a science fair for our class. We all got to present our own little experiments, from growing plants to making volcanoes erupt. It was a day filled with awe and discovery.

Benjamin, your scientific spirit teaches us to question, explore, and be amazed by the wonders of the world. Thank you for being our Scientific Explorer and helping us see the magic in everyday science!

Olivia

"*You are capable of doing amazing things.*"

Olivia is the artist with a heart full of joy. Her love for creating beautiful art and spreading happiness reminds us to find beauty in the world around us.

Olivia's art is like a ray of sunshine! Whether it's painting, crafting, or creating beautiful drawings, she brings color and happiness to our lives.

Olivia often organizes art sessions where we all get to create beautiful masterpieces together. She's like our art teacher, guiding us with her creativity.

Olivia organized an art gallery day for our class, and we got to display all our amazing artwork. It was a day filled with colors, laughter, and creativity.

Olivia, your joyful art reminds us that beauty and happiness can be found in creativity. Thank you for being our Joyful Artist and filling our days with colors and joy!

Jackson

"You are loved, you are precious, and you are enough."

Jackson is our class's caretaker, always looking out for others and making sure everyone feels loved and included. His kindness and empathy show us the power of friendship and being there for one another.

Jackson's caring heart is a beacon of kindness! Whether it's comforting a friend, including others in games, or sharing snacks, he makes everyone feel special. He has a collection of stuffed animals in our classroom that he shares with everyone. Each one has a special name and a story, and they remind us of the comfort of friendship.

Jackson started the Caring Friends Club where we all took turns being extra caring and kind to one another. It was a day filled with smiles, hugs, and friendship.

Jackson, your compassionate nature shows us that friendship and kindness make our days brighter. Thank you for being our Compassionate Caretaker and reminding us to care for each other always!

Emily

"Your imagination has no limits. Dream big and let your creativity soar!"

Emily is our class's storyteller extraordinaire. Her love for creating magical tales and bringing her imagination to life reminds us of the wonders of storytelling and the power of imagination.

Emily's stories are like magic! Whether it's creating fairy tales, adventure stories, or mysteries, she transports us to enchanting worlds with her words.

Emily often shares her stories with the class during storytime, and it feels like we're on a grand adventure every time she reads.

Emily organized a magical story quest for our class where we all became characters in her enchanting story. It was a day filled with imagination and wonder.

Emily, your storytelling talent reminds us that with a little imagination, we can go on incredible adventures. Thank you for being our Sweet Storyteller and sharing the magic of your words with us!

Aiden

"Every day is a chance to learn something new. Embrace the adventure of discovery!"

Aiden is our class's thoughtful thinker. His love for asking questions, pondering mysteries, and exploring ideas reminds us of the joy of learning and discovering new things.

Aiden's inquisitive mind is like a treasure chest of knowledge! Whether it's asking "why" and "how," sharing interesting facts, or sparking conversations, he keeps our minds buzzing. He has a collection of fascinating books about the world, and he often reads interesting facts to the class. He's like our resident encyclopedia!

Aiden organized a question challenge for our class, where we all got to ask a "big" question about the world and find answers together. It was a day filled with wonder and discovery.

Aiden, your thoughtful thinking inspires us to ask questions, seek answers, and explore the world. Thank you for being our Thoughtful Thinker and sparking our curiosity!

Harper

"Happiness is a choice, so choose to be happy and spread joy wherever you go."

Harper is our green-thumb gardener. Her love for nurturing plants and watching them grow reminds us of the magic of nature and the importance of caring for our environment.

Harper's green fingers are like magic wands! Whether it's tending to the classroom plants, learning about different flowers, or showing us how to grow our own, she brings the beauty of nature to our lives.

Harper organized a blooming garden party for our class where we all got to plant our own flowers and learn about the magic of growth. It was a day filled with blossoms and wonder.

Harper, your love for nature teaches us to appreciate the beauty of the world around us. Thank you for being our Little Gardener and sharing the magic of growth with us!

Thank you so much...

"You are like a puzzle piece that fits perfectly in this world. You belong, and you matter."

Dear Wonderful Friend,

Thank you for joining us on this heartwarming journey through the lives of these remarkable young heroes. We hope their stories have warmed your heart and inspired you to see the magic in everyday kindness.

As you close this book, we invite you to carry the spirit of these virtues with you. May you approach each day with open-heartedness, curiosity, and a commitment to make the world a better place. Remember, every small act of kindness has the power to create a brighter, more compassionate world.

Embrace the virtues that have illuminated these pages, and let them guide you on your own adventures. Live each day with kindness, and watch as the world around you transforms in beautiful ways.

Thank you for being a part of this journey. We believe in the goodness that resides in every heart, and together, we can spread a little more light in the world.

With warmest wishes,

Chivuzo

Who was your favourite pet?

_____

What are the things you love about your favourite pet?

_____

_____

_____

_____

_____

Did you have a great time reading about these amazing pets?

They are all wonderful, and there are so many beautiful things that we can learn from them.

Now we know that we too can be kind, brave, creative, honest and more.

But what do all these mean?

Well, let's take a moment to learn more about these virtues.

Kindness

Kindness is a magical superpower we all have, and it's about making the world a warmer, happier place.

It's like when you share your favorite snack with a friend who forgot theirs or help a classmate pick up their crayons when they accidentally drop them.

Kindness is when you see someone feeling sad, and you give them a big, comforting hug to make them feel better. It's the feeling you get when you do something nice for someone, like leaving a cheerful note on your teacher's desk to say, "You're the best!" or drawing a colorful picture for your mom to show her how much you love her.

Kindness is like sunshine on a cloudy day; it brightens everyone's hearts.

Curiosity

Curiosity is like having a treasure map to discover amazing secrets about the world around you.

It's when you look up at the sky and wonder why it's blue, or why birds can fly and you can't.

Curiosity means asking questions, like "How do plants grow?" or "What do ladybugs eat?" You might love exploring your backyard to find tiny creatures or listening to your grandpa's stories about when he was little.

Being curious helps you learn, and it's like having a never-ending adventure in your mind.

It's like being a detective, always on the lookout for cool clues about life!

Friendship

Friendship is like a big, cozy blanket that makes you feel warm and happy. It's when you have special pals who love playing games with you and sharing their toys.

Friends giggle together, help each other when things are tricky, and have awesome adventures.

Imagine having a friend who saves a seat for you on the bus because they want you to sit with them. That's friendship!

Friends make you feel like you belong and that you're important. It's like having a team of superheroes who are always there for you, ready to go on fantastic adventures and make memories.

Bravery

Bravery is like wearing a super-hero cape on the inside. It's when you face something a little bit scary or new and don't give up.

Think of when you tried riding a big bike for the first time without training wheels. That took real courage!

Bravery is when you're afraid of the dark but still walk into your room at night, ready to chase away the spooky monsters. Or maybe you were brave when you raised your hand in class to answer a question, even if you weren't sure if you were right.

Bravery is a heart full of courage, and it's what makes you feel strong when you need it most.

Respect

Respect is like using your kind words and your best manners to treat others just the way you want to be treated.

It's when you listen carefully when someone is talking, and you don't interrupt. When you show respect, it's like giving everyone a high-five, saying, "You matter, and I value you!"

Imagine when you're playing with your friends, and you let them choose the game they like because you want them to be happy. That's showing respect. It's also like saying "please" and "thank you" when you ask for something or when someone does something nice for you.

Respect is like a secret code for being a good friend and making people feel important.

Gratitude

Gratitude is like sending a huge "Thank You" hug to the world. It's when you feel really, really happy and thankful for the nice things people do for you.

Just think about your mom making your favorite snack, like peanut butter and jelly sandwiches, because she knows you love them. When you say "Thank you" with a big smile, that's gratitude.

Or when a friend shares their toys with you and makes your playdate super fun, saying "Thank you" shows how much you appreciate them.

Gratitude is like sprinkling kindness on all the good things in your life. It's a bit like having a thankful heart that spreads happiness.

Honesty

Honesty is like a shiny truth-telling superhero cape. It means telling the truth, even when it might be a little hard.

Imagine you accidentally broke your sister's favorite toy, but you tell her right away. That's being honest.

When you're honest, it helps you build trust with your friends and family. It's like making a promise to your heart to tell the truth, even if it's tough, like saying "I'm sorry" when you make a mistake.

Being honest helps you be a superhero of trust and good friendships.

Forgiveness

Forgiveness is like making peace with your heart and giving someone a friendly hug, even when they made a mistake.

Imagine your friend bumped into you by accident, and they say, "I'm sorry." Instead of staying upset, you say, "It's okay, I forgive you."

That's forgiveness! It's like giving someone a second chance and being ready to forget about what happened.

Forgiveness is a special way to make your heart feel lighter and your friendships stronger.

Determination

Determination is like having a never-give-up spirit that helps you reach your dreams. It's when you don't stop trying, even if something is really tough.

Imagine practicing a new dance move over and over until you get it just right. That's determination!

Determination is what makes you say, "I can do it," even when you're facing a challenge. It's like having a secret superhero cape that keeps you going until you reach your goals.

Perseverance

Perseverance is like being a brave superhero who never gives up, no matter how hard things get.

It's when you keep trying, even if it takes a long time. Think of learning to tie your shoes or ride a skateboard. It might take a lot of tries, but you don't give up.

Perseverance is like a superhero's superpower of patience and determination. It's what helps you get better and stronger, one step at a time.

Keep going, and you'll see that you can do amazing things!

Patience

Patience is like having a superpower of calm and waiting with a smile. It's when you don't get frustrated if things take a long time or if something doesn't happen as quickly as you'd like.

Imagine waiting for your turn to play on the swings at the park. Patience is when you wait your turn and cheer for your friends as they swing high in the air.

It's a bit like being a nature explorer watching a flower bloom slowly. Patience helps you stay peaceful and understanding, even when things don't happen right away.

It's like a secret superhero cloak that keeps you feeling relaxed and happy.

Love

Love is the warm, fuzzy feeling you get when you care a lot about someone or something.

It's like a heart full of happiness and kindness. Love is when your mom gives you a big goodnight hug and says, "I love you to the moon and back."

It's also when you cuddle with your pet or draw a beautiful picture for your best friend. Love is when you share your favorite toys and enjoy playing together, making everyone's hearts smile.

Love is a magical superpower that fills the world with happiness, and it's like having a heart full of colorful balloons that float with joy.

Cheerfulness

Cheerfulness is like being a bundle of joy and sharing happiness with everyone around you.

It's when you wake up in the morning with a big smile and say, "Today is going to be a fantastic day!"

Cheerfulness is like making your favorite game even more fun by laughing and giggling with your friends. It's a bit like having a pocket full of sunshine, ready to brighten even the cloudiest day.

Imagine when you sing your favorite songs, dance to the beat, and make funny faces to make your family laugh - that's cheerfulness! It's like a happiness superhero who spreads smiles wherever they go.

The End